V·I·S·I·O·N·S

Quilts of a New Decade

EIGHTY-THREE QUILTS FROM THE EXHIBITION

VISIONS—A NEW DECADE

Deborah Bird Timby, Editor

C & T Publishing

Many thanks to Bill Timby, my husband and my interface with the computer age, for his invaluable help. — Deborah Bird Timby

The artists retain the copyrights on all individual works shown in *Visions—Quilts of a New Decade*

Editing by Deborah Bird Timby
San Diego, California

Copyediting by Sayre Van Young
Berkeley, California

Design/Production Coordination by Bobbi Sloan Design
Berkeley, California

Photography by Carina Woolrich
San Diego, California

Typesetting by Byron Brown/MACAW
Oakland, California

Front Cover Quilt by Glenda L. King
Back Cover Quilt by Michiko Rice

Printed in Singapore

Published by
C & T Publishing
P.O. Box 1456
Lafayette, California 94549

Library of Congress Catalog Card No. 89-82562
ISBN 0-914881-27-2

Acknowledgments

It is with great pleasure that Quilt San Diego presents "Visions—A New Decade," an international, juried quilt exhibit that will be on view from May 19 through July 15, 1990, at the Museum of San Diego History in the heart of Balboa Park. The exhibition is accompanied by a series of workshops, public lectures, docent tours, and a wearable art fashion show.

"Visions—A New Decade" is an idea conceived in 1985 when San Diego quiltmakers decided to organize a juried quilt exhibit. We wanted to showcase to the community the outstanding quiltmaking we were seeing amongst ourselves. Our desire was to promote quiltmaking as the art form we knew it to be.

Thus, Quilt San Diego, a nonprofit organization, was born. Quilt San Diego's board, executive officers, and committee members are all volunteers—a "family" of quiltmakers and friends—who enthusiastically organized this exhibit plus many other quilt events.

Special recognition goes to Rose Turner, our "visionary," who saw it all in her mind's eye before we did; Patricia Smith, whose promotion made this exhibit international; and Lynn Johnson, the Exhibit Co-chair and Quilt San Diego Vice President, whose behind-the-scenes effort keeps Quilt San Diego operating.

A special thanks to Debra Casho of the San Diego Historical Society and to Carolie and Tom Hensley, C & T Publishing, for also strongly believing in our "vision."

Thanks to Deborah Timby, who willingly took on the challenge of book editor, and to Sharyn Craig for her continuing support.

My gratitude to my fellow Quilt San Diego board members: Rose Turner, Chair, Kate Besser, Linda Hamby, Lynn Johnson, Carol O'Brien, Patricia Smith, Deborah Timby, and Karen Wooton, and to our husbands, for their positive encouragement and understanding.

Grateful acknowledgment is given to

Hoffman California Fabrics

and to

RJR Fashion Fabrics

for their support in

quiltmaking activities

and for underwriting

Quilt San Diego's preparation of

Visions—Quilts of a New Decade.

◆◆◆

Dedication

We dedicate this exhibition to all San Diego quiltmakers who have supported us in reaching our goal, and to the quiltmakers worldwide who challenged themselves to enter "Visions." Their extremely high-quality entries ensured an outstanding exhibit.

We have been fortunate to have many fine people comprising our various committees and involved in our activities, people who have worked tirelessly to produce this exhibit, especially the Quilt San Diego committee chairpersons: Martha Brown, Barbara Friedman, Patti Garretson, Kim Graf, Shirley Greenhoe, Nancy Johnson, Maggi Kaplan, Harriet Love, Pat Marean, Sandy Patterson, Donna Rasmussen, Diane Seaberg, Gay Sinclair, Angela Smith, Julia Zgliniec, and Edith Zimmer. ◆

Arlene Stamper
President
Quilt San Diego

San Diego Historical Society Perspective

The San Diego Historical Society proudly welcomes Quilt San Diego's second juried exhibition. As a local and regional historical society, our mission is best fulfilled when we are able to encourage the understanding of the bonds that exist between our modern lives and the world of history.

Jonathan Holstein reminds us that quiltmakers today work in an environment of design and thoughtful craftsmanship reaching back in unbroken succession to America's earliest days. The quilts in "Visions—A New Decade" are visible proof of his thoughts, linking their creators with thousands of quilters whose patterns and techniques evolved into one of American's truly great indigenous art forms.

Quilts are natural vehicles for interpreting our connection to the past. Considered now primarily as works of art, they also recall family and home—our personal histories. Because of this, quilts are emotionally accessible to viewers in a way that other fine arts media are not. Contemporary quilt artists go beyond providing us with the pure visual pleasure of simply looking at something beautiful. They are sharing with us new insights, new views of our world.

The thought, skill, and care pieced into each quilt is matched by the tremendous effort Quilt San Diego brings to the development of the Visions project. Special thanks to Arlene Stamper and Lynn Johnson, Exhibit Co-chairs, and to the dozens of tireless volunteers who worked for over two years planning every detail of the exhibit.

In addition to "Visions," the Museum of San Diego History is exhibiting 19th- and early 20th-century quilts documented by the California Heritage Quilt Project during a statewide search. We believe the concurrent presentation of these two significant exhibits allows visitors to explore the nature of the human spirit of creativity—past and present—and to celebrate with us its bright future. ◆

James Vaughan
Executive Director
San Diego Historical Society

Introduction

Quilt San Diego proudly presents "Visions—A New Decade," an exciting international quilt exhibit. Bringing these magnificent quilts to San Diego may seem unusual. People perhaps think of San Diego as a beach community or as that little town south of Los Angeles. However, in the last decade, San Diego has emerged as a major center of cultural activity encompassing quilting as well as other fine arts and theater.

Quiltmaking in San Diego mirrors a nationally evolving pattern. Two major national events were catalysts for a quilting renaissance in the United States. A 1971 exhibit, "Abstract Design in American Quilts," held in New York City at the Whitney Museum of American Art, provided the forum for quilts to gain long-deserved artistic credibility. Then, the United States Bicentennial renewed interest and activity in colonial crafts and traditional home arts. Quilts gained popularity in the late 1970s and local adult school officials responded to the demand for quilting classes. Increasing numbers of students

encouraged the growth of quilt guilds and quilt shops which then offered more specialized classes.

By the early 1980s, two separate annual quilt shows were being held in San Diego County: the International Quilt Show, running from 1980 to 1984, and the San Diego Quilt Show, which began in 1981 and still continues. These shows not only highlighted local quiltmakers' work, but also invited nationally prominent quilters to teach or lecture. Heightened awareness of artistic quilts and the growing sophistication of local quilters prompted a special 1982 exhibit, the Friendship Quilter's Guild Show, a one-time presentation of guild members' and invited artists' quilts.

In the midst of the 1980s dynamic expansion of quilting, Quilt San Diego was formed to increase public awareness of quilts as a traditional and a contemporary art form. Support of these goals came from members of more than a dozen guilds encompassing an area twice the size of Rhode Island. Quilt San Diego's immediate goal was to organize an exhibition of

contemporary quilts of national scope. Always respectful of the importance of traditional quiltmakers, Quilt San Diego encouraged the display of quilts reflecting innovative uses of traditional patterns as well as original design. This philosophy culminated with a four-day juried exhibition in 1987, also called "Visions," featuring 83 quilts chosen from 352 entries from the United States and Canada.

Inspired by the enthusiastic response to that 1987 exhibit, Quilt San Diego promptly began plans for "Visions—A New Decade." The San Diego Historical Society invited Quilt San Diego to utilize their spacious museum facilities to present a major, two-month long, international juried exhibition. A distinguished panel of jurors, Jonathan Holstein, Jean Ray Laury, and Jan Myers-Newbury, spent two intense days selecting 83 quilts from 877 entries. Quilts from Australia, Canada, England, Japan, West Germany, and twenty-three states in the United States compose this highly regarded collection. ◆

Jurying Philosophy

Many of us who go to quilt exhibitions wonder how the quilts we see happened to have been assembled as a group. The quilts shown in "Visions—A New Decade" were selected by a panel of jurors who received instructions from Quilt San Diego. Prior to seeing any entry slides, the Quilt San Diego jurors read and discussed the following "Visions" jurying philosophy.

Quilt San Diego believes that quilts can be works of art. We define a work of art as one which does not copy another, but is in some way extraordinary and expressive, inviting us to see ourselves and the world in a new way.

Our exhibition should represent the current range of styles of quiltmaking. Many, if not most, quiltmakers work at a midpoint on the continuum between traditional and contemporary styles. It is not our intention to shock the public by exhibiting *only* the most avant-garde. We want to explore the creative process which includes both the traditional quiltmaker (who is not duplicating the past, but is taking a middle ground adapting time-honored designs and techniques) and the "experimental" quiltmaker (who is pushing the limits of the medium). It is important to represent the diversity of today's quiltmaking. It is equally important that each quilt stand on its own merits while affecting the other quilts in such a way as to provide an exhibition that "jells."

The general public should see quilts which look familiar and quilts which make the viewer stop, think, feel an emotion, or have an opinion.

We want quilts flowing with color, sparkling with wit, making visual impacts of great proportions, or having such subtlety that one must look closely to see the marvelous technical skill, unusual use of fabric, or the artistic methods used to create the design.

Quilts that make you laugh and sing and quilts that sober you—all those wonderful, incredible quilts that speak from the heart of the quiltmaker—we want the very best in quiltmaking today! ◆

The Jury

JONATHAN HOLSTEIN

Helping to jury "Visions—A New Decade" gave me a welcome chance to see the best efforts of contemporary quiltmakers. In addition, I always have a few particular interests to explore. My questions are: what links with the past are contemporary quiltmakers maintaining? Where are complete breaks into a new aesthetic occurring? Are old and new quilts judged successfully by the same aesthetic criteria? And the perpetual question, what about taste and judgment? In none of these areas was I disappointed for answers.

The range of work was quite amazing, from literal copies of early quilts to quilts which take the medium in very new directions. In between were many quilts informed by the past but very much updated: savvy interpretations of the inheritance. I was staggered and delighted by the extraordinary quality of both design and craft in quilts of all types.

I had a chance to check the question of aesthetic criteria while on the firing line. Having served on three-person juries for both historic and contemporary quilt exhibitions, I can say that the dynamics and statistics of such juries, one to the next, are startlingly similar. After the first several screenings, the same percentage of quilts seem to be eliminated or chosen. In addition, the jurors, who brought very different tastes and backgrounds to the process, ended in basic agreement a surprisingly high number of times. This seems to me quite amazing, especially here, where we picked approximately one-tenth of the entrants for the exhibition. Quiltmakers might like to know that no single perception, taste, or ideology governed this selection; it was completely democratic and fought out in the best democratic tradition.

JONATHAN HOLSTEIN, Cazenovia, New York. A quilt collector, historian, lecturer, and writer, Jonathan Holstein curated the 1971 Whitney Museum exhibit, "Abstract Design in American Quilts," which stimulated interest in quilts as a design form. He has since assembled many museum exhibitions internationally, and has written numerous exhibition catalogs, articles, and books, including Kentucky Quilts 1800–1900 and The Pieced Quilt. He has been active in historical quilt searches in New York, Texas, and Kentucky.

And there's always some give and take over personal favorites.

This is what I particularly like about the quilts I saw:

The wonderful use of color. Clearly, color experimentation is a prime interest of contemporary quiltmakers.

The many extremely successful modern interpretations of traditional designs.

The vigorous and innovative design sense we saw in many quilts. To me this appears part of a (not unexpected) trend towards more sophisticated design, more mature formulations of older ideas, and easier, more comfortable manipulations of the form.

It was only the limits imposed by available exhibition space which caused us sorrow; shows have to stop somewhere, but it often hurts. This was certainly the most painful cutting I have ever had to do, and near the end there is no telling what deal the dark powers might have cut with me for twenty-five more slots. Some quilts that I liked extraordinarily just couldn't go in. Jurors are, of course, paid to be ruthless and take the heat; you can blame them for anything you don't like about the show. I will be happy to accept any of that criticism since the necessary cutting left me with a considerable burden of guilt to work off.

I think we chose a smashing exhibition, a tribute not to our sensibilities but to the remarkable quality of the almost 900 entries. ◆

JEAN RAY LAURY

JEAN RAY LAURY,
Clovis, California. A full-time free-
lance artist, Jean Ray Laury has
shown quilts in numerous one-woman
and group shows in museums and gal-
leries nationwide. An author of nine
books, Ms. Laury's best-known works
are The Creative Woman's
Getting-It-All-Together at Home
Handbook, The Adventures of
Sunbonnet Sue, *and* Ho for
California: Pioneer Women and
Their Quilts, *a presentation of his-*
toric California quilts. Her popular
workshops and lectures reflect her wis-
dom, humor, and creativity.

The quilts in this remarkable collection offer visions of quiltmakers' perceptions and ideas, their fantasies and private worlds, and glimpses of secrets. Their cityscapes and skyscapes soar into imagined space or settle into backyard flowerpots.

A narrative of contemporary quiltmaking emerged from the slides we viewed, juxtaposing the traditions of geometric precision with innovation, freedom, or abandonment. Richly quilted surfaces and exotic hand-painted fabrics expanded the dimensions of quilt design. A tremendous commitment of energy, time, and concentration turned these visions into realities.

The task of choosing from hundreds of exceptional quilts the few to be singled out for inclusion was difficult. Because we were jurying not from the quilts themselves, but rather from submitted slides, sometimes the quality of the transparencies presented obstacles to the selection (distracting backgrounds or foregrounds, poor exposure, distorted colors, or shadows falling across the quilt). Fortunately, we were not encumbered by personal bias towards the artists' reputations since we did not know any of the makers' names while viewing the slides.

It was a privilege to join two jurors whom I admire and respect who so articulately offered insights and responses. Competition for "Visions" was formidable, submissions top-notch, and the exhibition will be one of the most outstanding this country has been offered. ◆

JAN MYERS-NEWBURY

Jurying "Visions" was a pleasantly difficult undertaking. As a group, we were unanimous in our praise of the range, skill, beauty, and impact of the quilts in the slides we viewed. If our task had been one of rewarding all quilts of merit with inclusion in this show, it would have been a considerably larger exhibit. Having myself been "rejected" from two juried shows in 1989, I know that no amount of "juror-speak" alters the disappointment that the "thin envelope" represents. We may understand the jurying process intellectually and know that the numbers alone dictate that less than ten percent get the "fat envelope" of acceptance. Nevertheless, this knowledge never really clothes us in the proper emotional armor. No juror is unaware of the human effort and aspirations represented by each work.

Some points describing the process itself seem relevant: three jurors spent sixteen hours viewing and reviewing nearly 900 anonymous entries. All were seen at least twice; many were seen as many as ten times. A great deal of discussion accompanied all but the first screening. Successive showings frequently altered our perceptions: some works with initial impact did not stand the test of time; some "sleepers" edged their way into more and more noticeable positions. I believe this system of successive viewings and re-evaluation is far superior to a scoring system where numbers are crunched and a cut-off made at "quilt 83." There were works I fought for and lost; this was true for all three jurors. A surprisingly small number of our decisions were unanimous and I was struck by the great benefit of having three viewpoints.

An issue of quilt competition that continues to confuse is that of influence and derivation. What, exactly, is "original work?" As is the

JAN MYERS-NEWBURY, Pittsburgh, Pennsylvania. An innovative quiltmaker, Jan Myers-Newbury uses only fabrics which she dyes in evenly-stepped value gradations of particular hues. Her distinctive quilts have been in many one-woman and group shows, including several in Quilt National. Her pieces are part of many museum and corporate collections. She lectures and teaches widely about design, color, and fabric-dyeing techniques.

case with other art forms, quilting has a unique set of parameters that seem to define "quilt." A tradition exists in which much variation in both technique and design has already been explored. The manipulations of colored bits of fabric invite comparison to various schools of painting: all the way from Impressionism to hard-edge color field painting. Various systems for organizing the unlimited possibilities are taught by quilt teachers internationally. It is crucial for a creative life to involve new learning, new influences, and a thorough historical perspective. For this exhibit, I looked for works representing a link to the quilt tradition (I think a quilt should look like a quilt), yet clearly stated that the maker had imposed her/his vision and experience upon elements derived from that tradition.

Basic principles of color and design represented by the submitted work were impressive. Stunning optical illusions and luminous effects were created through manipulations of color and shape. Fabric surface alteration (dyeing and painting) has now become commonplace, and the enterprising quilter is no longer limited to the whims of the fabric industry. This begs the inevitable question, "Where does 'quilting' end and 'painting' begin?" Dyeing, painting, stitching, and beading techniques are in the public domain; their use must be a means to an end if they are to be successful. In the best works, the whole was greater than the sum of the parts.

It is wonderful that our task was such a difficult one. I extend my encouragement and congratulations to all who submitted entries. "Visions" represents the best in quiltmaking today. ◆

The Quilts

Ann M. Adams
San Antonio, Texas

Blown Away
49 ½" x 44 ½"

Cotton, silk, polyester; polyester batting.
Hand dyeing, machine piecing, heat-fusible appliqué, machine quilting.

Juror's Choice:
Jean Ray Laury

This is the first quilt in a series using the tornado as a metaphor. I'm interested in the link between culture and fabric and the way in which certain fabrics are "read" by society. For example, a hierarchy exists suggesting that cotton, silk, and linen are in "good taste" and polyester is tacky or "low class." Fabric styles and patterns are important considerations to me for what they say. Two schools of design influencing my work are the Wiener Werkstätte and the contemporary Italian designers of the Memphis school. ◆

Carol Adleman
Coon Rapids, Minnesota

Wish You Were Here
58" x 48"

Hand-dyed cotton; polyester batting. Hand dyeing, cyanotype on fabric, machine piecing, hand quilting.

This quilt reflects a "life experience"—being on the beach in Nassau. With camera in hand, I am always on the lookout for striking but uncomplicated forms and patterns. When I begin working with a photo, I try to express the feelings of being there. I want to make it more than simply a blueprinted picture. Just for fun, on the back of the quilt, I sketched myself sitting in one of the beach chairs. ◆

Charlotte Warr Andersen
Salt Lake City, Utah

Paradise Lost
69" x 81"

Cotton, cotton/polyester, polyester,
silk, lamé, rayon; cotton batting.
Machine piecing, hand appliqué,
hand quilting.

Saltair was an enchanting resort built in 1893 on the shore of the Great Salt Lake. Designed by the architect of the Mormon Tabernacle, Saltair burned to the ground in 1926 and was replaced a year later by a less graceful and more ponderous building. I visited the second Saltair as a small child shortly before it was permanently closed in 1959 and have fond memories of it. A third Saltair, also an aesthetic disappointment, had been standing only two years before it succumbed to rising lake waters. I have given up my youthful fantasies of becoming fabulously wealthy and rebuilding Saltair in all its former beauty and grandeur. This quilt is the reconstruction of the Saltair of my dreams. The quilt border is made of two traditional blocks: The Xquisite and Lady of the Lake, appropriate subtitles for the quilt. ◆

Françoise Barnes
Colorado Springs, Colorado

Petite Misumena
60" x 60"

Cotton, cotton blends.
Machine piecing; hand quilting by
Susan Hershberger.

Nature is the first and foremost artist and art teacher; never any disappointment there! From my early childhood I have been fascinated by the natural world, especially insects and flowers. Insects, undeniable masterpieces of nature, provide flamboyance, geometry, and symmetry in one neat package. My quilt insects are not specific kinds, but rather are imaginary, dreamlike creatures with mysterious names. The series, "Misumena," a name related to spiders, is a tribute to all the exquisite insects whose intricate beauty would simply ravish us if only we could really open our eyes. ◆

Joan Basore
San Anselmo, California

Homeward Bound
79" x 74 ½"

Commercial cotton, hand-dyed and hand-painted cotton, cotton and metallic quilting threads; polyester batting.
Machine piecing, hand quilting.

For many years I have watched the migration cycles of shore birds near my home. Each time the beauty of their flight stops me in my tracks. Because I feel a deep connection to the natural world, birds have become a metaphor for expressing some of these feelings in my quilts. The particular inspiration for this quilt was a photograph in an article about San Francisco Bay's vanishing wetlands. The quilt is my expression of the powerful urge to return to our homes and places of refuge, a poignant feeling because some of us, both birds and humans, have no homes at the end of the flight. Nevertheless, the flight is a beautiful thing. ◆

Linda Liu Behar
Lexington, Massachusetts

In Winter's Woods
93" x 66"

Cotton, cotton blends, rayon.
Machine strip-piecing variation,
machine quilting (some by Susan
Bickford).

What excites me the most about quiltmaking is the richness of color and pattern that can occur by accidental juxtapositions of pieces of fabric. I want to take advantage of those serendipitous random happenings, but find that even with crazy piecing, too much conscious decision-making gets in the way. This quilt is my first try at a new technique, a sort of modified strip-piecing. In this case, the strips are woven together to achieve my rough design. As the quilt progressed, what I had thought of as tall mountains dissolving into mist became a wintry forest—another example of allowing chance to lead the way. ◆

Susan G. Bengtson
Pleasanton, California

Amish Weave
91" x 76 ½"

Cotton; polyester batting.
Machine piecing, hand quilting.

I enjoy puzzles of all kinds and the challenge of finding their solutions. Producing this optical illusion in fabric was great fun for me and a satisfying achievement. This quilt was inspired both by an Irish Chain variation in David Pottinger's *Quilts from the Indiana Amish* and by a student's quilt in Roberta Horton's Amish II class. The hint of a weave appeared in one of these quilts and I was determined to see if I could complete the illusion. Making the pieced strips "weave" required six values of color from light to dark and used about thirty fabrics. A special thanks to Roberta, for issuing this challenge. ◆

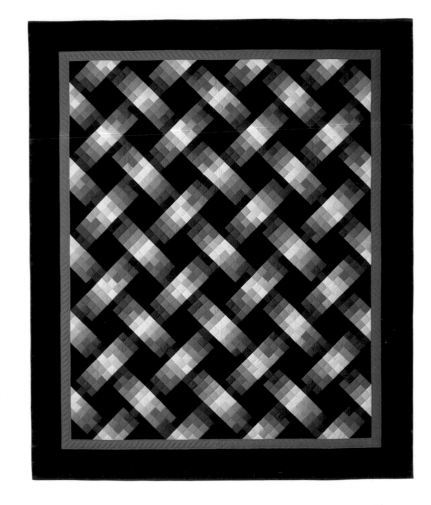

Sue Benner
Dallas, Texas

Autumn
73" x 73"

*Commercial cotton, painted cotton
and cotton blends; polyester batting.
Hand painting, machine piecing,
hand quilting.*

Year after year I am fascinated by the changing seasons. Although this is a much-used theme, I feel I still have more to say on the subject. As with each of the other quilts in my seasons series, "Autumn" is based on a nine-patch format and uses both commercially printed fabrics and ones I have painted. I incorporated my reactions, thoughts, and feelings about the season and depicted aspects of nature. With the changing colors and falling leaves, "Autumn" releases the tension after a long, hot summer. It is a time for settling in and rededicating myself to my work. ◆

Gayle Bryan
Hayward, California

Borrowed Blossoms
58" x 58"

Cotton; polyester batting.
Machine piecing, hand quilting.

We tend to pay much attention to the graphic quality of our quilts, backing away and squinting to view them. This is especially true of a simple pieced quilt like "Borrowed Blossoms." The multicolored quilting, the scale, and the complexity of the quilting design create a second layer of pattern, drawing the viewer back into the surface. "Borrowed Blossoms" is from a series of twenty-five quilts, all using the same block and set to explore color and abstraction. ◆

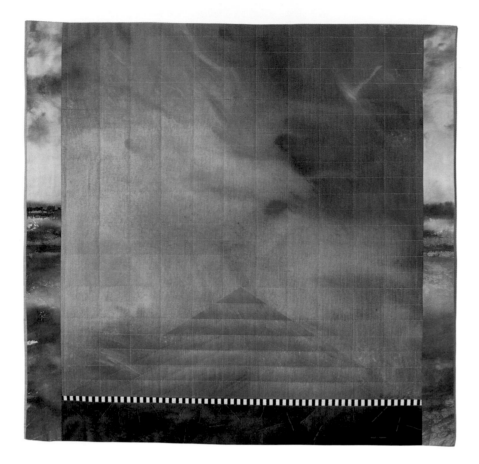

Elizabeth A. Busch
Bangor, Maine

Nightwatch
40" x 41"

Cotton canvas, muslin, commercial
fabric, acrylic paint, procion dye,
cotton embroidery floss,
Prismacolor® pencil.
Hand painting, airbrushing,
machine piecing, hand quilting,
drawing.

Beginning with "When We Were Young" (Best of Show, Quilt National 1989), I have made a series of quilts relating to the power of the triangle as a geometric shape, visual statement, and symbolic form. I worked on "Nightwatch" and several other pieces at once, pushing the triangle through extremes of color and angles. The triangle in "Nightwatch" is quiet and soft, but strong in its symmetry, alluding to a pyramid. The piece is about the summer of 1988 at the Haystack Mountain School of Crafts in Deer Isle, Maine, and the impact of this special place which pulses with creative energy emanating from the very granite upon which it is built. ◆

Joyce Marquess Carey
Madison, Wisconsin

Glad Rags 5, 6, 7
54" x 108"

Satin, velvet, silk, metallic fabric,
lamé, corduroy.
Machine piecing.

"Glad Rags" are fabrics about fabrics; each of the three is a cheerful gesture like waving a kerchief, pennant, or flag. I designed the first of the series originally for a children's hospital so I could help the kids feel happier by making a more cheerful environment. They make me happy, too— especially when someone says, "Those aren't flat, are they?" (Yes, they are!) ◆

Joyce Marquess Carey
Madison, Wisconsin

Red Squares
45" x 45"

Jacquard-woven Chinese portraits,
satin, metal badge.
Machine piecing, machine-stitched
trapunto.

"Red Squares" is the second in a series of political cartoons. Recently, I came across a supply of jacquard-woven portraits from China. I've been wanting to incorporate pictorial material in my work and these photo-realistic fabrics are perfect. All of the portraits are of former Communist leaders. I am not a political animal, but I do love puns, visual and otherwise. After I had thought of the title "Red Squares," the piece designed itself. ◆

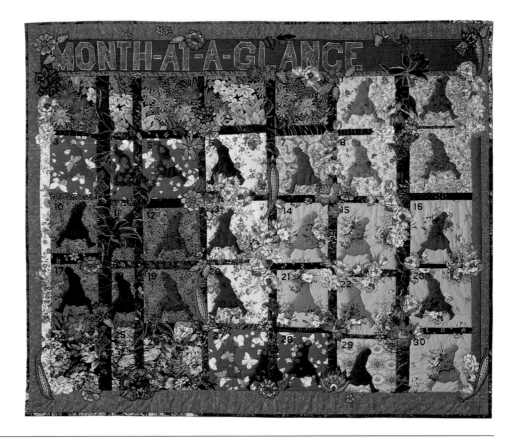

Barbara Carow
East Walpole, Massachusetts

Month-at-a-Glance
57 ½" x 68"

Cotton, beads; polyester batting.
Screen-printing with fiber-reactive
dyes, machine piecing, machine
appliqué, hand quilting, beading.

I'm concerned about the many pressures on young women today, as they are encouraged to "have it all" and, in the process, do it all. This quilt represents fantasy vacations which help women make it through the month. The image of the woman is adapted from a photograph by John Blanding in the *Boston Globe*. ◆

Erika Carter
Bellevue, Washington

Descending
76 ½" x 43"

Cotton; cotton/polyester batting.
Machine piecing, hand appliqué,
hand quilting.

My primary interest in quilting is color and texture. Nature often inspires my imagery, which I express through the use of color, pattern, and piecing. Part of a series on trees, "Descending" suggests the trees and ferns of the Pacific Northwest during the summertime. ◆

Carlene Chang
Berkeley, California

Delectable Mountains II
78" x 90"

Cotton, cotton blends.
Machine piecing, hand quilting.

With this quilt I tried to create a stage set. It is a doorway into another world, a leafy, sunlit jungle beyond an arch. The light of the stage spotlights seems to come from above; the sudden darkness of the orchestra pit is at the bottom. ◆

Stephanie Randall Cooper
Everett, Washington

Thika
60" x 63 ½"

Cotton, rayon, acetate; polyester
batting.
Machine strip-piecing, machine
quilting using sew-and-flip method,
hand-tied knots.

"Thika" is the second piece in an ongoing series. I was inspired by a book describing pioneering in Kenya during the early 1900s. The lives of these people on the surface appeared calm and ordinary, but upon deeper examination were revealed to be more complicated and intriguing. I refer to this in my design by creating a multidimensional illusion. By using a square-within-a-square block and selecting conflicting versus harmonious fabrics, I interrupted the emergence of strong vertical lines with competing horizontal strips. ◆

Wendy Lewington Coulter
Clearbrook, British Columbia,
Canada

A Piece of the Pie
70" x 58"

Cotton; cotton batting.
Color photocopy transfer, machine
piecing, stamping, hand quilting.

In my quilt, I deal with some of
my fears and frustrations with the
current environmental crisis.
I created pieced "pie" blocks with
color photocopied "fillings" representing aspects of our threatened
environment: plants, animals,
space. I placed these natural
images in a very rigid, "chopped
up" context because for me this
represents the way humans view
Earth as a consumable commodity
to be exploited at random, rather
than as an interdependent whole
to be cared for at all costs. I like
the pie image for several reasons:
its obvious relationship to the
expression "get your piece of the
pie"; its connection with pie graphs
and dividing a whole; plus its relationship to domestic experience—
how we all contribute to the fate
of our planet by the choices we
make as consumers. The outer
border is quilted with a chain pattern representing the interdepen-
dence of all living things. ◆

Barbara Lydecker Crane
Lexington, Massachusetts

Cataclysm
41" x 77"

Cotton, some hand-tinted or hand-painted.
Hand piecing, machine piecing,
hand appliqué, hand quilting,
machine quilting.

I hope this work will take the viewer on a journey into the unknown, charged with both excitement and uncertainty. "Cataclysm" refers to my belief of how life first came into being through natural forces and evolution, and also through some unseen but real force that articulated the first protozoan from its neighboring plankton. I seek to celebrate this power. ◆

Nancy Crasco
Arlington, Massachusetts

Katsuji Wakisaka
39" x 54"

Cotton, cotton blends, fabric paints;
polyester batting.
Machine piecing, hand painting,
hand quilting.

The exotic landscape of "Katsuji Wakisaka," which takes its name from a ten-year-old piece of Marimekko fabric, is one of a continuing series of experiments with surface enhancement of quilt tops. After sewing together a top from commercially printed fabrics, I add cohesive design elements using a limited palette of Deka® fabric paints. I "draw" the landscape only after the basic forms are determined by the fabric placement. When the drawing-painting on the top is completed, I finish the quilt in the traditional manner. ◆

Lynn J. Crook
Berkeley, California

The Purple Square
62" x 62"

Cotton; polyester batting.
Machine piecing, strip piecing, hand
quilting.

This quilt design grew from a basic, but enlarged, sawtooth grid. I tried to capture the effect of sunlight streaking across a dark space. I used strip piecing to create vibration between contrasting colors. The purple squares were added to simplify the initial design and enhance the diagonal light effect. ◆

Deborah Ellen Davies
Osterville, Massachusetts

Cold Fusion
75" x 75"

Cotton, linen, cotton blends, rayon;
cotton batting.
Machine piecing, strip piecing,
machine quilt-as-you-go.

In this work I experimented with cool colors and fused geometry with a sharp accent on the circle. The quilt was conceived and constructed during the recent scientific controversy regarding molecular cold fusion. While the scientific jury remains divided on the merits of their version, I like to think that my "cold fusion" experiment concludes nicely. An antique cobweb quilt served as my point of departure for this modern design. The medallion is my instinct; I rely on the constant equilibrium which it provides. My fascination with this variant of the medallion emerges from the fact that so many straight lines can mimic these graceful circles. Experimentation begets discovery! ◆

Deborah Ellen Davies
Osterville, Massachusetts

Patterns of Solitude
58" x 58"

Cotton, linen, cotton blends, linen damask; cotton batting.
Hand piecing, machine piecing, strip piecing, hand quilting.

The floor plan of Michelangelo's St. Peter's Basilica is the inspiration for this design. Explicit in the creation is my desire to experiment with the challenge of the curve. My "library" of fabrics and scraps provides continual stimulation and an abundance of reference material. I typically plan my work on paper first, but the true creative expression ensues with the juxtaposition of real fabric textures and colors. As always in my work, I hope to convey a sense of beauty, and in this piece specifically, the positive air that solitude can provide. ◆

Gayle Earley
Burlingame, California

On Another Level:
In Another Space
58" x 58"

Cotton, cotton blends.
Machine piecing, strip piecing,
machine quilting.

I'm fascinated by the spontaneity and uninhibited use of color and design in Afro-American quilts that seem to explode with the sheer exuberance of life itself. I find that constructing a few quilts in this quick and playful manner is wonderfully freeing and fun. Using no templates, I begin making these quilts with just a basic overall design, starting in the center and working my way out. I construct large squares and triangles by strip piecing the bold prints, stripes, and color gradations I like so well; then I measure and cut them to the size required for the next section. It's more deliberate than the Afro-American style and the choices become more difficult as I move farther from the center. It's such fun combining these wild fabrics in unique combinations and stepping back to marvel at the unpredictable results. ◆

East Bay Heritage Quilters
Albany, California

Baltimore Album Redone
95" x 95"

Cotton.
Hand appliqué by thirty members of
East Bay Heritage Quilters,
Albany, California; hand quilting
by Crazy Quilters and members of
East Bay Heritage Quilters.

This quilt closely approximates an antique Baltimore Album Quilt in the Metropolitan Museum of Art in New York. It was made as a display piece for the East Bay Heritage Quilters' Symposium in 1988, held at Mills College in Oakland, California. Adele Ingraham used a magnifying glass to draft the pattern from the Museum quilt poster and served as coordinator and supervisor of the planning and construction. Except for one block made by two people, a different person made each block. A mini-group, the Crazy Quilters, quilted it with help from members of East Bay Heritage Quilters. ◆

Rosemary Elkes
San Diego, California

Yellow Flowers
42" x 55"

Cotton, cotton blends, gold metallic thread.
Machine piecing, hand appliqué, hand painting, machine quilting.

Years ago I saw a magazine picture of a floral painting and the image stayed with me. When I needed a quilt for a special place in my home, I recalled the painting and made a quilt which reminded me of the picture. Parts of the quilt are painted: areas of fabric which were too plain or too white, I painted with a blue wash. ◆

Caryl Bryer Fallert
Oswego, Illinois

**Chromatic Progressions:
Autumn**
96" x 88"

*Cotton; cotton/polyester batting.
Machine piecing; pleating, twisting;
machine quilting.*

This is the eleventh quilt in a series in which three-dimensional, constructed tucks are incorporated into a pieced background. Cotton fabrics dyed in color progressions are used to construct two-sided tucks; one progression forms the front side of the tucks while a second is used on the back. A third set of graduated colors creates the background of interlacing arcs and the border. The intersecting color progressions and the texture of the twisted tucks create the illusion of foreground motion. Colorful arcs are juxtaposed against a rather static background pieced in shades of brown and grey. The browns and muted colors suggest a crisp, sunny autumn day. The traditional quilt block (Dove in the Window) on the back of this contemporary art quilt is my tribute to the creativity of anonymous quilt artists of the past. ◆

Mary Fogg
Merstham, Surrey, England

Blue Tower, a Woollen Scrap Quilt
87" x 70"

Wool, cotton, wool couching thread.
Machine appliqué, couching, machine quilting.

The inspiration for this quilt comes from the fabrics. The textures and colors of tweeds and other woven woollens, in all their variety, give me a sensuous pleasure that I want to share with the viewer. I apply and quilt the patches by machine stitching over a woollen couching thread; then I fringe the overlapping edges. The fringed edges, part of the structure of the cloth, are normally hidden when the material is used conventionally for clothes or furnishings. I display them openly to give extra light and shadow to the quilt surface. ◆

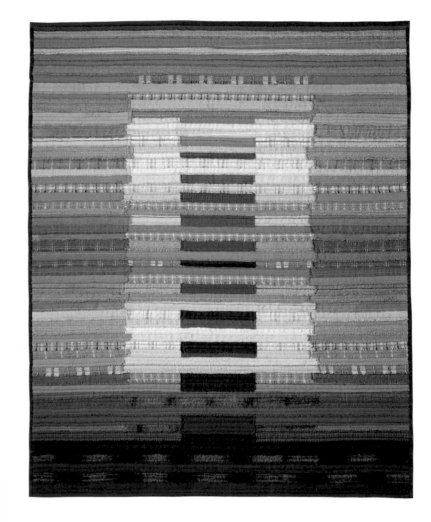

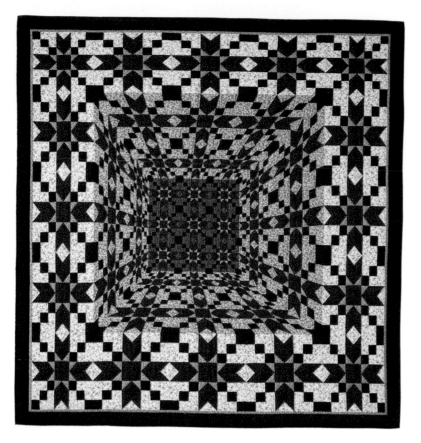

Bobbie Fuhrmann
Lancaster, New York

In Depth
80" x 73"

Cotton; polyester batting.
Hand piecing, hand quilting.

I always enjoy creating innovative interpretations of traditional
designs. "In Depth" combines
approximately 3000 pieces to
give a three-dimensional look to
the traditional Stepping Stones
pattern. It was a difficult quilt
to piece because the middle
portion is off-center; each piece
in the dimensional area is a different size and shape. The design
had to be drafted full-size onto
graph paper and then cut apart to
make templates for each piece in
that area. The quilting brings
out additional geometric shapes
to enhance the patchwork
design. ◆

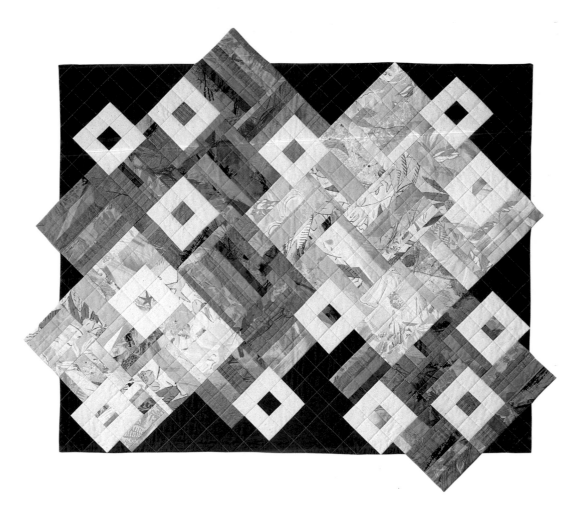

Ruth Garrison
Tempe, Arizona

Plane Dealing
51" x 59"

Cotton; cotton/polyester batting.
Machine piecing, machine quilting.

In designing "Plane Dealing," I tried to create an illusion of overlapping planes tossed onto a dark ground. The open squares, scattered across the top, give a view to the layers beneath. Piecing all the elements into one plane—the quilt top—provided an absorbing puzzle. My purpose in making quilts is to create interesting, stimulating, and increasingly complex images. My desire is for my quilts to stand on their own visually, without additional explanations or analysis. ◆

Fiona Gavens
Whiteman Creek, New South
Wales, Australia

Australis
72 ¾" x 80 ¾"

Cotton, cotton blends.
Machine piecing, machine quilting.

This quilt was made specifically for a quilt exhibition celebrating Australia's bicentenary. Through my use of color, I wanted to emphasize the tremendous diversity of landscape, vegetation, and climate in this country. By blurring and abstracting the shape and definition of the map, I hope to convey a movement between past, present, and future. The piecing shape is a "one-patch" of my own design. "Australis" is part of a series in technique, not in design. ◆

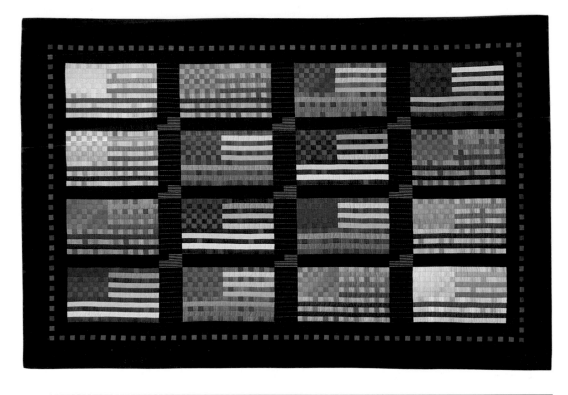

Carol H. Gersen
Boonsboro, Maryland

Squares and Bars
52" x 77"

Commercial cotton, hand-dyed cotton; cotton/polyester batting. Machine piecing, hand quilting, machine quilting.

I began this quilt during the last weeks of the 1988 Presidential election campaign, with a heightened awareness of flags as a design form in American art and in possession of about 4000 tiny fabric squares left over from another project. I finished the quilt in February 1989, well before the Supreme Court decision on the desecration of the flag and the subsequent controversy. ◆

Carol H. Gersen
Boonsboro, Maryland

Rivers in the Sky
72" x 72"

Commercial cotton, hand-dyed cotton; cotton/polyester batting. Machine piecing, strip piecing, hand quilting.

This is one of the first quilts I made after learning to dye fabric. I chose blue because I knew that my dyed fabric would be very wash- and light-fast. Past experiences made me wary of commercially-dyed blues which for me tend to fade. The block is a greatly simplified log cabin, part of which I strip-pieced. Upon completion, the overall effect resembled a landscape with a blurred middle ground connecting rivers and sky. ◆

Helen Giddens
Mesquite, Texas

Fan Lover
84" x 84"

*Commercial cotton, hand-dyed
cotton.*
Machine piecing, hand quilting.

Pattern and movement excite me and I hope it shows in my work! This particular piece was inspired by the designs I saw created while looking through a kaleidoscope. The colored stones and glass bits play visual games, sometimes appearing to be familiar objects. The image I saw looked like fans swirling as in an Oriental dance. I tried several variations before designing "Fan Lover." The background pattern crowding the fans' movement produces the rhythm and repetition which I like to incorporate in my quilts. ◆

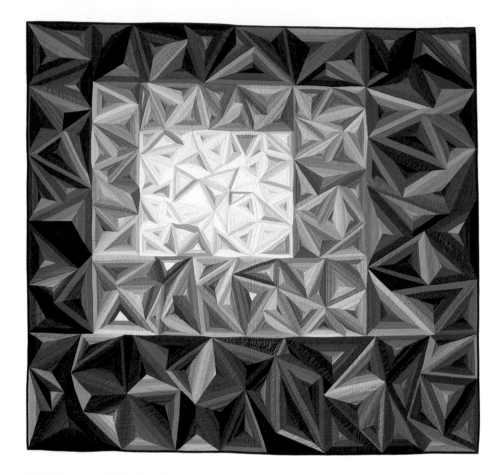

Alison Goss
Hockessin, Delaware

Looking for the Inner Light
84 ½" x 90"

Cotton; cotton/polyester batting.
Machine piecing, strip piecing, hand
appliqué, hand quilting.

This is the first of a series based on strip-pieced triangles, exploring color and design possibilities and reflecting my concern for the environment. "Looking for the Inner Light" represents a meditative process of looking inward, overcoming the distractions and problems of the outside world, and finding inner peace. I am convinced that we all have unique, creative visions hidden inside ourselves that we need to find ways to reveal and to use. ◆

Gail Hanson Greengard
Minneapolis, Minnesota

Carnaval en Mitla
32" x 72"

Silk; polyester batting.
Machine piecing; construction and
quilting in the same step by machine
using a process called string quilting.

In the past the patterns I used have always been my original designs. Inspired by the many beautiful antique quilts being shown now, I thought it would be fun to apply my own colors and arrangements to a traditional pattern, in this case the Virginia Reel block. I chose this pattern because in it the colors swirl and spin, especially where the complementary colors meet. The color scheme is two spectrums interwoven at right angles. My trips to Mexico inspired the quilt's colors, pattern, and name. The colors are like the bright, flashy costumes of the pre-Easter *carnaval* parades and the block pattern is very similar to the stone mosaics on the ruins at Mitla. Thus the name, "Carnaval en Mitla." ◆

Carol Anne Grotrian
Cambridge, Massachusetts

Lacrimosa...Gloriae
62" x 66"

Hand-dyed cotton.
Hand dyeing, machine piecing,
hand quilting.

"Lacrimosa...Gloriae" is my interpretation of Mozart's Requiem. The measured progression of chords in the "Lacrimosa" finds its counterpart in the quilt's horizontal and vertical bars. The stretched harmonies of the music and the colors of the dyed fabrics are kindred. Both contrast with the next movement, "Domine Jesu Christe! Rex Gloriae!," which sings out just as the light shines through the bars of the quilt. The Requiem as a whole is filled with passages of affirmation offsetting the overall ponderous theme. I made this quilt for the Musical Medley Competition as part of Quilting-by-the-Lake Conference in Cazenovia, New York, where it received first place in the classical music category. "Lacrimosa ...Gloriae" is my first return to light beam transparencies since finishing "Light of Liberty," my entry for the Great American Quilt Festival. ◆

Sandra K. Harrington
Anchorage, Alaska

1988
48" x 48"

Cotton, fabric paints, permanent marker.
Hand painting, machine piecing, pulled threads, unfinished seams turned to surface, machine quilting.

The year 1988 was a time of emotional crisis for me and my family. Since I approach my work intuitively, I believe my quilt "1988" is an artistic response to the events which significantly affected my life and yet over which I had no control. The fabric is painted and marked in images unique to me—they are my signature—while the unfinished seams and loose, hanging threads are more universal design elements.

For me, they refer to those times when one feels mired in tangled events that invade one's life and leave one with feelings of being exposed and slightly frayed along the edges. ◆

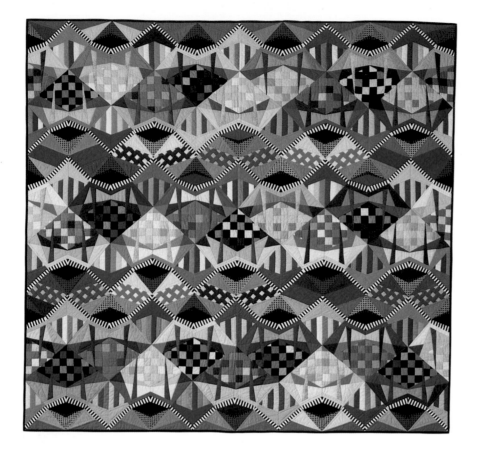

Sharon Heidingsfelder
Little Rock, Arkansas

Colorful Applause
70" x 72"

Cottons, some hand-dyed and silk-screened.
Machine piecing, hand quilting.

"Colorful Applause" is part of my melody series of quilts. I am intrigued with the rhythm of repeated patterns as well as with diverse color combinations. I always use black and white in my quilts because I just like their starkness against the colors. Like many other quilters, I work with quilts simply because of the satisfaction of handling fabrics, choosing colors, and designing. ◆

Bonnie Bucknam Holmstrand
Anchorage, Alaska

Night Blooms (In a Crystal Gazing)
82" x 58"

Commercial cotton, cotton blends, some hand-dyed; polyester batting. Machine piecing, strip piecing, hand quilting.

This block design was inspired by a photo of a hedgehog cactus flower. The strip-pieced fabric in the center of the quilt represents the thorny spines of the cactus. Background colors are those I have seen in the desert when a storm is gathering. The khaki and earth tones of the land and vegetation are juxtaposed with the bright blue sky as it is over-taken by the grays and purples of the approaching storm. ◆

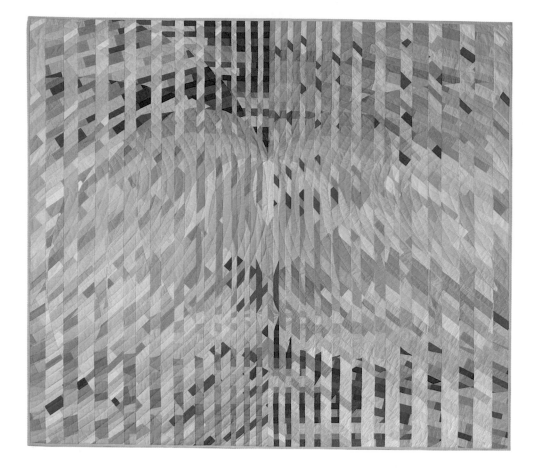

Inge Hueber
Cologne, West Germany

Valentine
66" x 75"

Hand-dyed cotton; cotton batting.
Hand dyeing, machine piecing, strip
piecing, hand quilting.

This quilt is an expression of the joy and happiness in my life with the heart as a symbol of love. Red, turquoise, and yellow in many hand-dyed shades represent these feelings. My use of Seminole technique adds movement and vibrations. In Germany, quilts do not cover us during cold nights, but a quilt on a wall may add warmth to our hearts! ◆

Marcia Karlin
Lincolnshire, Illinois

Garden at Dawn
44 ½" x 53"

Cotton and silk, hand-painted and cyanotyped; beads, sequins. Machine piecing, hand quilting, machine quilting, hand embellishing.

My work often blends pictorial elements with abstraction so that a variety of viewpoints reflects different levels of experience. "Garden at Dawn" was originally inspired by a black-and-white photograph of picotee petunias, but the image that evolved suggests an elusive dream garden. I wanted to create a shifting sense of light and shadow with textures and colors depicting blossoms, leaves, soil, water, and sky. This is not the neat, manicured garden of the landscape designer; rather, it is a fragment of nature with its order and chaos and the inevitable growth, change, and decay. ◆

Marcia Karlin
Lincolnshire, Illinois

Blue Garden I
41 ½" x 76"

Cotton, primarily cyanotype and inkodye prints; net, organza. Cyanotype and inkodye printing, machine piecing, machine appliqué, machine embroidery, machine quilting.

For me, creating a work of art is a process of discovery, rather than the execution of a preconceived idea in fabric. The cyanotype process inspires much of my work; I use it to produce blue-toned "photograms" that are particularly appropriate vehicles for expressing the themes that interest me. In "Blue Garden I," images of flora and fauna are suspended in an imagined environment that challenges conventional notions of time and space. The photograms symbolize memory while the color blue suggests space, infinity, isolation, and longing. My layering of visual elements is deliberately ambiguous in order to emphasize the sense of dislocation, estrangement, and fragmentation. ◆

Natasha Kempers-Cullen
Bowdoinham, Maine

**On a Clear Day You Can
See Forever**
66" x 42 ½"

*Cotton, cotton blends, fiber-reactive
dyes, metallic thread, glass seed
beads; polyester batting.
Hand painting with dyes and textile
ink, hand quilting, machine quilting,
beading.*

I was inspired to make this quilt
by my experiences during the first
few days of my new job at
Spindleworks, a sheltered workshop for mentally handicapped
adults. Everyone there was cheerful, curious, helpful, and eager to
engage in creative activity. There
were pots of geraniums on the
windowsills and color everywhere;
the handwoven items and the
drawings and paintings were sen-
sational and inspiring. I loved it!
I began this piece there in a work-
room, so the clients could watch
me working and sense what we
would be doing together in the
weeks to come. If only we can get
beyond ourselves, then we can see
in the midst of turmoil and sad-
ness in the world that there is also
beauty and clarity shining
through. This philosophy makes
life's difficulties bearable and gives
us moments of joy. ◆

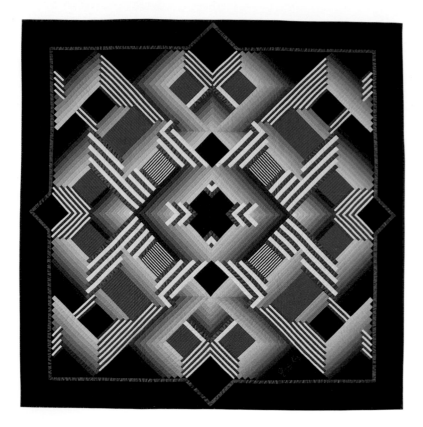

Glenda L. King
Lexington, Kentucky

LCC 3:9 (Structural Portents)
64" x 64"

Cotton, some hand-dyed, satin, cotton blends; cotton/polyester batting. Machine piecing, strip piecing, hand quilting.

JUROR'S CHOICE: JAN MYERS-NEWBURY

The second quilt of my "Structural" series, "LCC 3:9" draws on the timeless spirit of innovation. The design of "Structural Portents" is founded on traditional log cabin construction techniques, yet it pushes the tradition toward modern complexity. Its precise diagonal composition echoes the energy found in modern architecture. Like architecture, quilts provide both function and beauty; they also utilize contrasting materials, spatial symmetry and balance, and resolve their complexity in stability. Rather than building a traditional cabin with logs, I built "LCC 3:9" like a skyscraper, drawing upon traditional forms, techniques, and materials, but in the end reflecting the character of a technological age. ◆

Ann Kowaleski
Mt. Pleasant, Michigan

The Day of the Dead
78 ½" x 99 ½"

Cotton, cotton blends, corduroy, lamé, satin, wool; braid, ribbons, buttons, felt, beads, sequins, mirrors, textile paint, cotton and silk embroidery floss, horsehair, shells, fish spine.
Reverse appliqué, hand appliqué, hand embroidery, ribbon work, hand quilting.

This quilt is part of a series based on my travels to Mexico where one sees incredible colors in buildings, festivals, and everyday scenery. It depicts the Mexican holiday "Day of the Dead," which is somewhat like Halloween or All Saints Day. Death is present in many forms in Mexican custom as the fate that awaits all humans. The Mexicans seem to flirt with death, mocking it and treating it with humor, while still taking it seriously. During the weeks before the holiday, bakeries are filled with skeleton-like goods; the markets sell special masks. As a way of showing homage to the deceased, altars are decorated and provided with food, perhaps some flowers, and folk pieces. I like the concepts of making masks and of "putting on masks" as a way to perceive another reality. The characters in my quilt seem to take on personalities by themselves, becoming silent company. ◆

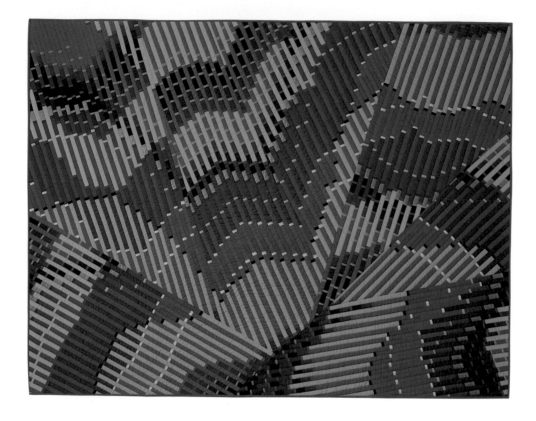

Judith Larzelere
Dedham, Massachusetts

Tempest
56" x 74"

Commercially-dyed cotton;
polyester fleece.
Machine strip-piecing; construction
and quilting in the same step by
machine using a process called string
quilting.

With "Tempest," I explored rhythm in a closely interlocking composition where one set of colored bands creates a fence-like screen through which can be seen the second color set. My personal concern was to stretch my customary color vocabulary and create works not based on nature observation. Tiring of the sure success of certain color combinations, I doubted that my creative development could proceed by using habitual choices. Working to overcome my inner limitations and working rules, and distrusting my intuitive selections, I forced myself to complete this quilt. It revolted me while I made it, and only after it was finished did it speak to me of new, inventive strength. The title "Tempest" describes both my state of turmoil during its creation and the completed image. ◆

Judith Larzelere
Dedham, Massachusetts

Magnolia
74" x 60"

*Commercially-dyed cotton;
polyester fleece.
Machine strip-piecing; construction
and quilting in the same step by
machine with a process called string
quilting.*

In early 1988, I suddenly became
aware of the arrival of spring to
Boston. Undamaged by frost or
rain, the magnolia trees that
year were particularly full and
spectacular. The cream, pink,
and plum colors of their blossoms
intoxicated me and I began
at once to transfer the color
rhythms and spacing of a bloom-
ing tree into cloth. The result is
"Magnolia." This quilt contains
movement of swirling and lifting
color as the life forces of spring
were recreated by my hands and
eyes. ◆

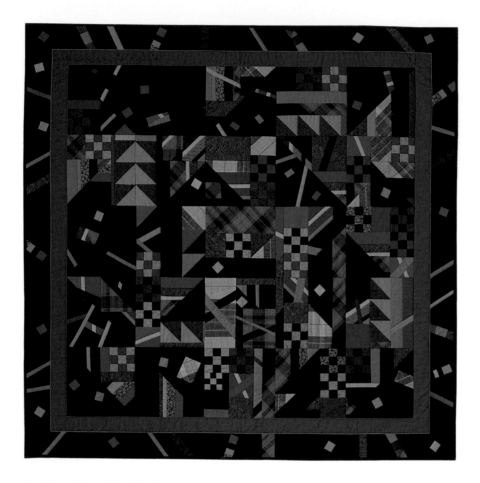

Susan Webb Lee
Greensboro, North Carolina

Purple Haze
53" x 53"

Cotton; cotton/polyester batting.
Machine piecing, machine quilting.

In "Purple Haze," I wanted to work with an asymmetrical format which would appear somewhat chaotic, yet still be coherent within the square. I selected predominantly dark colors which I use quite often, but for the first time introduced plaids to my fabric choices. I used two techniques learned in a workshop: "cut-throughs" and "edgings." ◆

Linda Levin
Wayland, Massachusetts

Pallone: Paese Dei Sogni
(Balloon: Land of Dreams)
50" x 77"

Hand-dyed cotton.
Hand dyeing using procion fiber-
reactive dyes, machine piecing.

Four hot-air balloon trips over Siena, Italy, inspired this work, one of a series. These flights offered me new opportunities to see the world differently. Aerial views are surprising and wonderful, sometimes reducing large areas of countryside to pattern, light, and shadow, and sometimes making the known look very strange indeed. This piece is based on a flight over the Siena Cathedral and depicts and repeats its architectural features in a very abstract way. It is a time of day when the light casts a golden glow over everything, and shadows are deep, dark, and mysterious; seen from the air, they seem to create a whole, other city in the midst of the solid, tangible buildings. ◆

Linda Levin
Wayland, Massachusetts

First Light
61" x 45"

Hand-dyed cotton.
Hand dyeing using procion dyes,
machine piecing.

With this piece I was particularly interested in controlling color in order to concentrate on other elements of design. So I restricted myself primarily to a range of grays and neutrals. I feel that the color range in "First Light" is very like the unreal, almost absence of color just before dawn. Since the design of the quilt is quite abstract, I rely on mood to convey the feeling I want to achieve. ◆

Linda Ruth MacDonald
Willits, California

Clear Palisades
92" x 92"

Hand-dyed cotton; cotton batting.
Hand dyeing using procion dyes,
machine piecing, hand quilting.

I wanted to create tension and interest by manipulating the visual laws of gravity. Bars of pattern are seemingly tilting and falling, yet some are flat, others three-dimensional, and some even seem to contradict their role in the picture plane. This landscape is completed by a binding layer of elaborate quilting in blue and yellow thread. ◆

Marguerite Malwitz
Brookfield, Connecticut

Frozen Sunset
40" x 61"

*Cotton, tie-dyed cotton, cotton
blends, silk, satin.
Hand piecing, machine piecing,
hand quilting.*

My quilts are inspired by my experiences with nature and by word-picture phrases from Scripture. "Frozen Sunset" was inspired by a spectacular winter sunset near our home. The hot pinks and oranges in the sky were reflected across the ice-covered lake. The boat houses and homes across the bay receded into the darkness of the mountain that hid the setting sun. Although the experience lasted only moments, it was etched in my mind for months and remained the motivation for making this quilt.

"Frozen Sunset" was also inspired by Job 37:10: "From the breath of God, ice is made, And the expanse of waters is frozen." ◆

Terrie Hancock Mangat
Cincinnati, Ohio

Broken Marriage Vessel
54" x 41"

Cotton, cotton blends, silk,
embroidery thread, beads, amethyst,
rosary, ostrich eggshell beads, plastic
leaves, paint.
Machine piecing, reverse appliqué,
hand embroidery, hand painting,
beading, hand quilting.

"Broken Marriage Vessel" is
about the process of divorce.
The vase represents the union,
which is torn in half; the
chartreuse half represents me,
while the black half represents
my ex-husband. The children are
shown half on each side, also
torn in two. On my side are the
symbols for art, Catholic heritage, nurturing (roses), healing
(amethyst), new growth (green
leaves), and headstrong individu-
ality (a black cat). On my ex-
husband's side are symbols for the
Sikh religion, Africa (ostrich
eggshell beads), money, flashy
cars, and surgical instruments
(with drawn blood). There is a
note of hope in the two bursts of
energy rising from the interior of
the broken vessel; two individual
spirits are being released to go on
to each one's own destiny. ◆

Merrill Mason
Jersey City, New Jersey

Night Gorilla
61" x 48"

Cotton, paint, buttons, metallic thread.
Shredding and sewing fabrics, rubber stamping, machine embroidery.

Several years ago I made an "Urban Gorilla Jacket," inspired by the handmade, shredded fabric dashboard rugs popular with the car-cultists in our inner-city neighborhood. It seemed to me that a gorilla lap robe would be a good next move. ◆

Merrill Mason
Jersey City, New Jersey

Tornado III
64 ½" x 52 ¼"

Cotton, silk, polyester, buttons, metallic thread.
Layering, machine piecing, hand painting with textile pigments, rubber stamping, color photocopy transfer, drawing with dyesticks.

For two years I have concentrated on a series of quilts using violent natural forces, particularly tornadoes and hurricanes, as metaphors for physical and emotional turmoil. I like contrasting the quilt, a symbol of women's work and domestic security, with a destructive and chaotic image. Women spend much of their lives trying to protect themselves and their families from chaos, while seeking structure and tranquility in a random world. The text on the front border (and continuing on the back panel of this two-sided quilt) is the testimony of a man who was run over by a tornado and lived to tell his tale. The text ends with a quotation from Ezekiel, the first recorded sighting of a tornado, describing "a fire infolding itself." The colors used in the front of the quilt refer to this. The loose grid and floating rectangle formats reflect the need for structure in chaos. ◆

Kathleen H. McCrady
Austin, Texas

Come Into My Amish Garden
73" x 68"

Cotton; cotton/polyester batting.
Hand piecing, machine piecing,
hand appliqué, reverse appliqué,
hand embroidery, hand quilting.

Inspired by a scrap quilt of over-lapping nine-patches set on point, I tried the same technique using solid "Amish" colors. After making a stack of nine-patches minus the one square, I arranged them on point, gradu-ating the values in each color, except where I changed the color entirely. The sky and ground are miniature log cabin blocks pieced of various blues and greens. The Amish gardens I have seen are vegetable gardens with borders of flowers. However, my quilt has flowers with a border of vegetables. ◆

Ruth B. McDowell
Winchester, Massachusetts

A Carpet of Goldthread
62" x 107"

Cotton, cotton blends, linen, rayon, permanent inks; polyester batting. Machine piecing, hand appliqué, hand quilting.

Nature continues to be a source of inspiration for me. In the past few years, I have focused my attention on trees; in this case, trees in the landscape of a New England forest. Goldthread is a very small wildflower which carpets the forest floor with dark green shiny leaves and tiny white flowers. I prefer to construct my quilts from "found" fabrics, usually commercially available prints. In "A Carpet of Goldthread," I was unable to find a satisfactory fabric for the trunk of the largest tree, so I made my own using permanent inks over a shaded furnishing fabric. ◆

Carol McKie-Manning / Christen Brown
San Marcos, California

Ivan's Magic Journey
52" x 44"

Silk, cotton, metallic fabric, polyester, embroidery floss, perle cotton, metallic thread, beads, sequins, buttons, appliqués, found objects.
Hand dyeing, hand appliqué, trapunto, hand embroidery, beading, hand quilting.

Our inspiration for this quilt evolved from a mutual love for illustrated children's stories. We were influenced by many books, particularly the illustrations of Ivan Bilibin's Russian fairy tales. We also have great appreciation for ethnic folk art and textiles and envisioned this collaboration as feeling like an Indian *kalaga*, a type of sequin-encrusted beadwork. ◆

Jeannette DeNicolis Meyer
Portland, Oregon

Worlds Collide
60 ½" x 49"

Hand-dyed cotton.
Hand dyeing, machine piecing,
hand quilting.

Inspired by an antique "Windmill" quilt, I began a "Windmills of My Mind" series. I wanted to play with motion and color, imagining windmills moving across the surface and through the color gradations. "Worlds Collide" is the third quilt in this series. This quilt incorporates three Trip Around the World structures. The first trip is colored symmetrically (shades of lime-green to turquoise) and depicts the spinning windmill blades. The other two trips (with values of gray) are symmetrical but off-center in the background. The two gray background worlds collide, forming a blinding flash. Many things came together in this quilt: thoughts about how we must learn to co-exist on this planet and what will happen if we don't; a self-dare to use a particularly strange run of dyed color gradations; and a decision to design this quilt on paper first rather than "on the wall" as I usually do. ◆

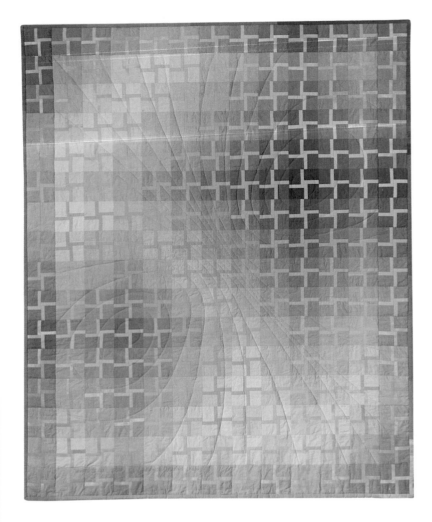

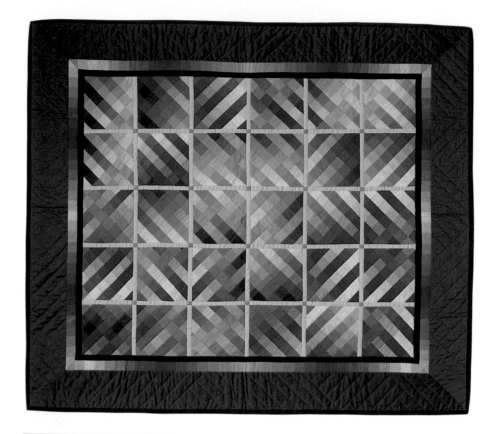

Mary Morgan
Little Rock, Arkansas

Phoenix
47" x 53"

*Hand-dyed cotton; cotton/polyester
batting.*
*Hand dyeing using fiber-reactive
dyes, machine piecing, strip piecing,
hand quilting, machine quilting.*

I enjoy using color gradations to achieve luminosity in my quilts. When I started this quilt, I intended it to be a tightly structured, symmetrical composition of small color-graded squares flowing smoothly from one hue to the next. But after assembling more than 1200 squares, I realized it was a disaster. Due to a tiny error in my strip-piecing template, the measurement along all four edges of my quilt was two inches larger than across the center. Worse, the design was unexciting.

Resisting the temptation to throw it all away, I decided to cut the quilt top into 7" squares and re-arrange the design to give it a more unpredictable feel. The result is a more exciting piece. Hence the title, "Phoenix." ◆

Susan T. Mosler / Rachel Beth Mosler
Barrington Hills, Illinois

Gemsticks
55" x 48"

Cotton, net, translucent fabrics, cotton and silk embroidery threads, bits of gemstones; cotton batting. Hand painting, hand appliqué, hand embroidery, hand quilting, machine quilting.

"Gemsticks" is the fourth quilt in a series celebrating my daughter, Rachel Beth. She is a magical child whose spirit transcends gravity and whose glowing respect for the natural world embraces her art. I have saved all of her drawings and relish their freshness each time I recreate them in fabric. "Gemsticks" is a grassy hill of happy children dancing freely among nature's little creatures, who, importantly, fly freely themselves. It is about reveling in nature and respecting its wonder. It is about believing in magic, tooth fairies, butterfly princess fairies, and yourself. ◆

Joyce Murrin / Jean Evans
Congers, New York; Medina, Ohio

Baskets Baskets
100" x 78"

Cotton, cotton blends, some hand-painted; polyester batting.
Hand appliqué, broderie perse, hand embroidery, hand quilting.

We are twins, quiltmakers with considerably different individual styles, who have made one quilt together each year for five years. This quilt uses the "baskets" theme of the 1988 American Quilter's Society show, where it won a second place ribbon in the group category. Being basket makers and plant lovers, we found it very easy to design this quilt. We chose the quilting designs in the border from the quilt itself, extending the flowers and other design elements into the border. ◆

Jean Neblett Nägy
San Francisco, California

Primal II
53" x 69"

Cotton, metallic thread.
Machine piecing, machine quilting.

Primal II uses a repeat block designed with sixteen, multi-curved pieces. Each piece is inset with printed fabric which creates a "brush stroke" or a feeling of organic growth. The quilting crosses lines, thereby further connecting and dissecting the blocks; it is free form and often takes the shape of symbols. Perhaps the most important element in my work is color. I intuitively elaborate on an idea and allow the design to develop spontaneously. The color may change many times before I feel it is right. ◆

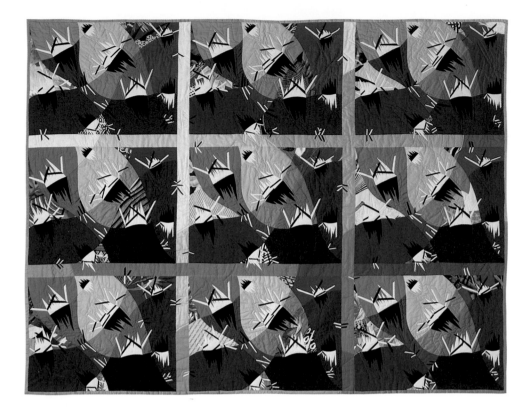

Jean Neblett Nägy
San Francisco, California

Primal I
58" x 75"

Cotton, Ultrasuede®.
Machine piecing, machine appliqué,
machine quilting.

Juror's Choice:
Jonathan Holstein

As a repeat motif, I designed this sixteen-piece, rectangular block incorporating irregularly curved lines. After piecing the blocks, I used Wonder-Under™ to heat-set Ultrasuede® to the quilt top before appliquéing each piece. There are one hundred pieces of appliqué in each block. A former dancer, I work with movement in my quilts, a fast and lively shifting of the eye and senses through color and shape arrangement. This process is very gratifying. Some pieces are sophisticated and elegant, others are elaborate, textural, and fun; all are joyous, which is my ultimate experience in creating. How they evolve and complete themselves is exciting and new with each event. ◆

Katie Pasquini-Masopust
Oxnard, California

Labyrinth
78" x 91 ½"

Cotton, satin, lamé, corduroy,
velvet.
Hand piecing, machine piecing,
reverse appliqué, hand quilting.

After reading a book on isometric perspective, I thought it would be a good design technique for my next quilt. Using isometric graph paper, I played with the possibilities of layers of units. Everything is based on 60 and 120 degrees, so it all fits together quite nicely. This design reminds me of a maze. I hand pieced most of this quilt—a first for me. I was in the process of moving, so hand piecing over 200 black units for the background gave me a creative outlet while my studio was in boxes. I am very excited about the possibilities of isometric perspective and plan to work with this design technique for some time. ◆

Sue Pierce
Rockville, Maryland

Hat Trick
42" x 60"

Cotton, cotton blends; polyester batting.
Machine piecing, machine appliqué, machine quilting.

Hats, hats, and more hats. Thirty-six machine appliquéd, fedora-like hats repeat across this quilt top mirroring every mood: a sophisticated party hat in black with pink tulips, a beige country-tweed with jaunty feathers, and even a pink flamingo tourist hat. You should be able to find just the right hat in this closet for every occasion. A multitude of fabrics (stripes, checks, calicoes) combine to create both a whimsical feeling and a country style. The stripped border and pieced binding hold this couturière collection together. ◆

Lyn Piercy
San Francisco, California

Enchanted Garden
94" x 76"

Cotton, cotton blends.
Machine piecing, hand appliqué,
hand quilting.

I wanted this quilt to look like a scene one would see while standing in a garden, a scene that is lush, green, and sprinkled with color. For a greater challenge, I decided to piece the flowers rather than to appliqué them. Using class meetings as motivation, I used some original designs and other traditional and published designs modified in various ways. The varied use of the striped fabric allows the flowers to float on the background. ◆

Jane Reeves
Canton, Ohio

Post Modern XX
64" x 96"

Commercial cotton, hand-dyed cotton; polyester batting.
Hand dyeing, machine piecing, hand quilting.

I make abstract, geometric, quilted wall-pieces, using color, line, and shape to create illusions of space and movement. I am particularly interested in the interaction of colors, tints, and shades so I hand dye many of the fabrics in my quilts. My concern is with formal issues of color, shape, and line rather than with content. I hope the viewer will be moved to ponder the difference between appearance and reality and the creation of order within chaos, ideas which I always consider when I work. ◆

Michiko Rice
Escondido, California

Compass Reflections
84" x 84"

Cotton; polyester batting.
Machine piecing, hand quilting.

In 1983, I attended a precision machine-piecing class. The technique I learned inspired me to make this compass quilt for my husband, who is retired from the United States Navy. It was fun to work with the many shades of blue, my favorite color. I hoped to create a cool, nautical image for this quilt for summertime use. ◆

Jane A. Sassaman
Chicago, Illinois

Information Radiation
65" x 65"

Cotton, cotton blends.
Machine piecing, machine appliqué,
machine quilting.

Currently, I am exploring the concept of "radiation." Radiation is typically a word with a negative connotation. Coupled with "nuclear," it becomes a phrase that terrorizes our world. But I have been considering other meanings of the word. Radiation can be divine or sublime, inspirational or expirational. Consider the radiation of the sun, of the soul, or of the spirit—all originating from a central source and reaching outward. "Information Radiation" refers to the overwhelming abundance of information in our lives; it is hard to separate inane from essential information. This quilt refers to the deceptive glamour of mass media permeating society as one mass consciousness, totally disregarding the individual. ◆

Joy Saville
Princeton, New Jersey

Opus in Red
86" x 85"

Cotton, silk; voile interlining.
Machine piecing; construction and
quilting in the same step by machine
using a process called string quilting.

"Opus in Red" is inspired by my
desire to explore one color. For
me, color expresses concepts and
feelings; the sheer glory of color
attracts me! There is a whole-
ness, a completeness about color
that reaches my very being. My
response is my work—a celebra-
tion, a dance, a song, a word, a
prayer, an attempt to express the
essence I experience. I have
developed a process of piecing in
which my focus is on the manipulation of color instead of on the
usual repetition of pattern and
color. During the process of
manipulation, color begins to
speak for itself. I listen. When I
hear it, I am transformed. ◆

Constance Scheele
Katy, Texas

When Twenty Seemed Old
67" x 78"

Cotton; nylon, silk, and rayon
threads; cotton batting.
Machine piecing, hand appliqué,
machine quilting.

When I was a young girl, I loved
to swing. Our swing was near a
lake and had long ropes so I could
swing high into the trees. When
I would swing, the colors around
me would fragment, giving little
glimpses of the surroundings. It
was a carefree time, when twenty
seemed old. Now, looking back
from the other side of twenty,
twenty seems very young. ◆

Sally A. Sellers
Vancouver, Washington

The Price of an Afternoon
60" x 47"

Commercial cotton, hand-dyed
cotton; cotton/polyester batting.
Hand dyeing, machine piecing,
strip piecing, machine quilting.

My title comes from this quote
by Dorothy Evslin in the book
A Mother's Journal:

"What is the price of an afternoon when a small girl is
soothed in your arms, when the
sun bolts through a doorway and
both you and the child are very
young?"

I have three young daughters at
home, one of whom is severely
handicapped; their needs are
great. I love them desperately,
but realize the need to nurture
myself in order to survive. I
therefore arrange times to be
alone to quilt. These times alone
are poignant, however, as I realize
I may be giving up such a perfect
moment as described in the quote
for the necessary solitude of my
work. It is a high price. ◆

Quote reprinted by permission of
Running Press Book Publishers,
Philadelphia, Pennsylvania.

Susan Shie assisted by James Acord
Wooster, Ohio

Back to Eden
80" x 78"

Fabrics, paint, dye, leather, three-dimensional appliquéd figures, quartz crystals, beads, cotton embroidery floss, buttons, fish scales; polyester batting.
Hand piecing, hand embroidery, hand painting, hand quilting.
From the collection of Darrel and Nancy Seibert, Silver Lake, Ohio.

This quilt is our first "Green Quilt," part of a global project to make quilts embodying the faith that Earth will be healed and balanced. Its central figure represents Copper Woman from the creation story of Vancouver Island natives. Below Copper Woman is the message "Learn from the Animals; Return Our Earth to a Peaceable Kingdom." Many elements in this quilt speak to our return to "Eden" via healing, love, forgiveness, and sharing. For example, two shrine doors cover hearts giving messages of healing. Personal totem animals (leather circles) flip over to reveal secret pockets. The quartz crystals on the quilt are healing stones programmed to give their vibrations to the Earth and to all her creatures. The green goddess, magic hummingbirds, and an earth turtle bring additional friendly energies for a balanced nature. ◆

Carol Soderlund
Geneva, New York

Covenant
75 ½" x 75 ½"

Commercial cotton, hand-dyed
cotton, cotton blends; cotton batting.
Hand dyeing, machine piecing,
hand quilting.

"Covenant" expresses my vision of our earthly condition. The title refers to God's promise to Noah, symbolized by the rainbow of color in the quilt. Although we are bound on earth by our own limitations, represented by the gray stone walls, the rainbow pierces through the gloom promising new life within and beyond our earthly boundaries. This work is part of a design series exploring woven effects and illusions of a third dimension. I used perspective and careful shading of more than one hundred fabrics (some hand-dyed) to create, without using any curved seams, the vision of a globe in space. ◆

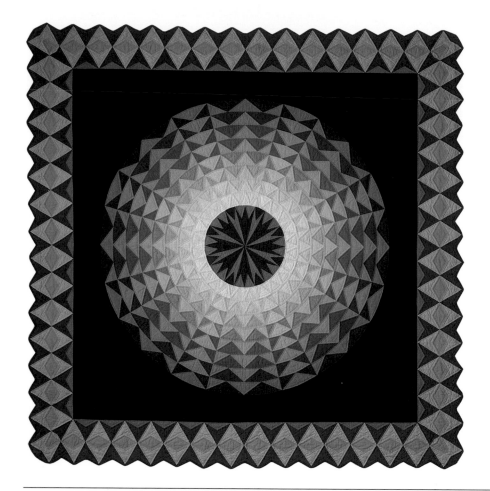

Judy Sogn
Seattle, Washington

Moonglow
82" x 81"

Hand-dyed cotton.
Hand dyeing using procion dyes,
machine piecing, hand quilting.

I designed "Moonglow" as an entry for the 1989 American Quilter's Society show, the theme of which was circles. My inspiration came from an antique quilt pictured in *America's Glorious Quilts*. I made many changes in both color and design to take advantage of the gradations of the hand-dyed fabrics. ◆

Michiko Sonobe
Tokyo, Japan

Flowering
84" x 84"

*Cotton; polyester batting.
Hand appliqué, stuffing, hand
quilting.*

Most of the quilts I make are very different from this one. I wanted to have at least one quilt with flowers on it. My husband painted a picture of flowers and the design of this quilt is based on his painting. To emphasize the graceful shapes of the floral sprays, I imitated their curves in stuffed-work feather plumes.

I contrasted the texture of the plumes by quilting the entire background with closely spaced diagonal lines. ◆

Arlene Stamper
San Diego, California

Koinonia Garden
62" x 94"

Cotton.
Machine piecing, hand appliqué,
hand quilting.

In Greek, *koinonia* means "very close fellowship." This word best explains my relationship with a special group of friends who have met to quilt every Tuesday for the past eight years—the Tuesday Group. This quilt is part of a friendship block exchange. I gave the North Carolina Lily pattern with a few fabrics to my friends and asked them to add other pastel materials. Later, when the blocks were sewn into a top, my friends helped me baste it for quilting. As each person's block came into my hoop for quilting, I thought how special that person was to me. "Koinonia Garden" has a joyful quality representing all the happiness my friends bring to me. Integrating the blocks through the quilting patterns, I used a water-soluble fabric marker to draw freehand curved lines from one Lily block to the next, crossing over seams as I went. Any unwanted lines, I just "erased" with a spray bottle and started over! The colorful rainbow ribbon border is emphasized by the weave and flow of the quilting design. ◆

Glenne Stoll
Denver, Colorado

Spring: Garden Series #1
56" x 53"

Cotton, metallic fabric; cotton batting.
Machine piecing, strip piecing, machine quilting.

Springtime in Colorado is mostly mud and late snowstorms. I designed this quilt in the dark days of February, when spring is a wonderful, although dimly remembered, dream of a time when color reappears in the landscape. The contrast is somewhat like Dorothy arriving in the land of Oz from the bleakness of Kansas. My aim in this quilt is to convey the feelings of anticipation and spontaneity. ◆

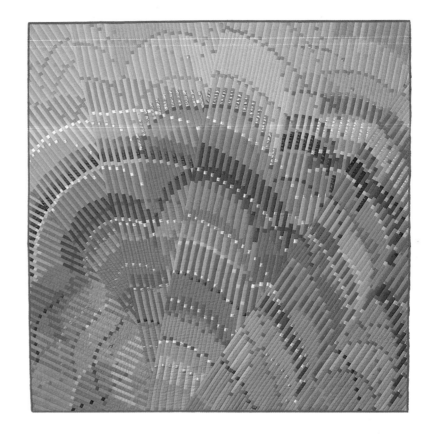

Nancy Taylor
Pleasanton, California

My Road to California
100" x 76"

Cotton, cotton blends; polyester batting.
Machine piecing, hand appliqué, hand quilting by Margaret Vantine.

My husband and I grew up in the Midwest and wanted to move to California. However, school and job changes took us first to Arizona and Texas, then Louisiana, and finally, eight years later, to California. The "road" in the center foreground reflects that journey. The bright colors at the top seem appropriate to depict the liveliness and diversity of our destination. ◆

Bonny Tinling
Vista, California

Open Windows: Dawn to Dusk
96" x 87"

Cotton; polyester batting.
Machine piecing, hand quilting.

This quilt was commissioned to reflect the style of Deirdre Amsden's "Colorwash" series of miniature quilts, but on a grander scale. About one hundred Liberty cotton prints are involved in creating the value gradations; many are turned to the reverse side to extend the value range. I realized after making this quilt that each day we have choices in perspective available to us. What we do with these choices and how they affect us are a reminder to keep open our own views. I plan to make a series of quilts based on other designs I drafted at the same time as this one, but in contrast to this large quilt, they will be smaller in scale. ◆

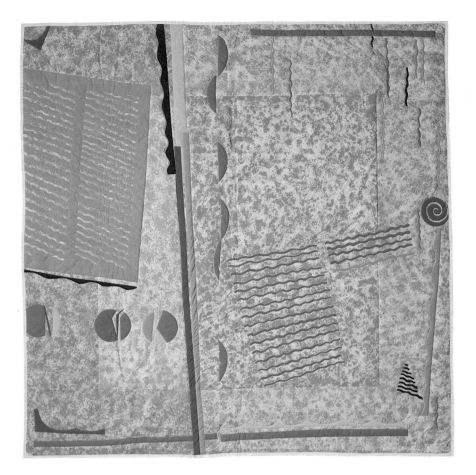

Ann Trusty
Lawrence, Kansas

Light Dance
72" x 72"

Cotton.
Hand painting, machine quilting.

The inspiration for "Light Dance" comes from a very special seasonal light effect. In late autumn and early spring, the late afternoon sunlight in the Hudson River Valley rakes across the river at a horizontal angle. The reflection from this light is cast upon my studio walls in the form of a golden dancing light. In this quilt, I capture the exquisite and fleeting "Light Dance." ◆

Emily Zopf
Seattle, Washington

Granite Quilt
38" x 63"

Cotton, fabric paints;
cotton/polyester batting.
Hand printing, machine piecing,
machine quilting.

"Granite Quilt" was inspired by the mosaic stone floors found in European churches. These mosaics often create the illusion of three dimensions. This led me to think about creating the illusion of stone from fabric. I printed my fabrics to look like granite and pieced them in a mosaic pattern altered to give the feeling of natural rock formations. ◆

Write for a free catalog of other

fine quilting books from

C & T Publishing

P.O. Box 1456

Lafayette, CA 94549